KU-648-096

Contents

# ⚠ PLAY IT SAFE!

It can be all too easy to get swept up in playing Pokémon, but it's always important to put safety first when playing. Unfortunately there are no real-world Pokécenters, so have a look at these tips to stay safe!

Always know where you're going and pay attention to your surroundings.

Never wander on to private land, buildings, or industrial areas without first getting permission. **If you're anywhere unfamiliar, you should always research the location before you proceed.**

Always make sure you are aware of the weather forecast and daylight hours. Weather can change fast and you can easily get caught out. This is especially the case in locations where the temperature can drop drastically after dark.

If you are venturing out into the wild, or into environments where weather and temperature can change suddenly (even if it seems like a nice day), **always have the appropriate clothing and gear, including proper trekking shoes.** Depending on what time of year and what kind of environment you are in, you should consider taking things like waterproof jackets, warm clothes, a flashlight, lighters or matches, and **enough water / food to last if you get stuck out in the night.** Even a real map and compass that is separate from your phone is a good idea. **Also note what kind of critters you could encounter,** this includes wild animals and domestic.

Let someone know exactly where and for how long you are staying out, and always stay on or near a noticable trekking path! (If a path fades off to a small or over-grown path, don't follow it.)

Never try to cross rivers, rocks, or cliffs that seem questionable or dangerous.

When you approach an industrial area or building, **look out for debris that can hurt you** and never go near anything that looks unsafe. Also, you should always notice what kind of condition a building is in before you enter, and never go anywhere that has a posted warning sign of any kind. They are there for a reason!

If you are in a city that is unfamiliar, always research where you are going and have enough coins to catch a bus or two!

Know the local emergency number and keep it in your contact favourites on your phone.

Younger players should never wander away from their parents, especially in large crowds.

But above all, if you use your common sense, you'll have more fun!

Disclaimer: We are not safety experts and have no formal training in safety or wilderness survival. The above recommendations are based on common sense practices but will not guarantee your safety while playing the game.

UNDERSTANDING YOUR SCREEN

Since you'll be spending a lot of time here, it's best to get used to what you'll be looking at.

Player Icon
Your Player Icon is your avatar's face in the bottom left of the screen. Tap on it to open up your player info, including your nickname, your team, start date, PokéCoins and your current experience points.

Pokéball Menu
There are four menus hidden within the Pokéball in the centre of the bottom of your screen.

Pokédex
This is where you can look at all the Pokémon you have both caught and encountered, and read more about their vital statistics, type and evolutionary chain. It also acts as a checklist of sorts to track your progress on how close you are to catching them all!

Pokémon
In this menu you can see all the Pokémon that you currently have, as well as eggs waiting to be hatched. Pokémon you have transferred back to Professor Willow do not appear here.

Items
This is your backpack, which holds all of the items you collect in the course of your journey.

Shop
Here you can trade PokéCoins for various items like Pokéballs, Incense and Lucky Eggs.

Nearby Pokémon
Your Pokémon tracker can be found by tapping the white rectangle in the bottom right of your screen.

TERMINOLOGY

Before you start your journey to become the best Pokémon Trainer with the help of this guide, it'd be a good idea to understand the Pokémon-specific words and whatnot we'll be using from here out.

CP (Combat Power)
A Pokémon's strength is displayed as its Combat Power (CP). CP helps determine how a Pokémon will fare in battle.

Eggs
Eggs are items that can be found at Pokéstops. There are three varieties that require different distances to be walked in order to hatch.

Evolution
Most Pokémon have an evolutionary chain. In Pokémon Go, giving a Pokémon special Candy can make it grow into a new, more powerful form of itself.

XP (Experience Points)
Every Trainer earns XP along their journey. Gaining XP means getting a higher Trainer level, which leads to different rewards and possibilities.

HP (Hit Points)
Hit Points (HP) measure a Pokémon's health. If a Pokémon's HP reaches 0, it will faint, and can no longer battle.

Candy
Candy allows a Pokémon to evolve and grow stronger.

Gym
Team-based where you can battle and claim it, or train and gain Prestige.

Incense
Attracts wild Pokémon to you.

Incubator
An item that is given to you by the Professor, or bought or collected in the course of the game. You need to put your Eggs in here if you would like to hatch them.

Lure Module
Attracts wild Pokémon to a Pokéstop.

Lucky Egg
An item that doubles the XP you earn.

EXPLAINED

There are going to be quite a few unfamiliar new terms, so take a second to look through this little glossary to familiarise yourself with what's ahead.

Pokéballs
Items required to capture Pokémon in the wild.

PokéCoins
A currency you can use to exchange for items in the shop.

Pokédex
Your comprehensive guide to all of the Pokémon you have caught or encountered.

Pokéstops
Special locations on the map that will give you items like Pokéballs, Eggs and Potions.

Potions
An item that can restore a Pokémon's HP.

Prestige
How a Gym's progress is measured.

Razz Berry
An item that when fed to a wild Pokémon, makes it easier to catch.

Stardust
An item used to Power Up Pokémon.

Training
Battling Pokémon at friendly Gyms in order to increase your XP and the Gym's Prestige.

Trainer
Pokémon Go players (psst, that's you!)

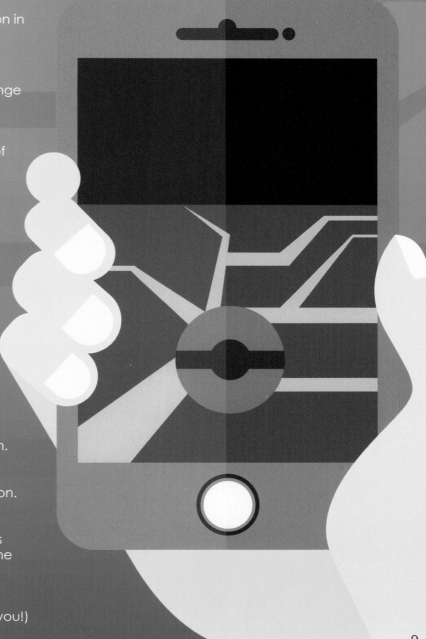

HOW TO CATCH YOUR

As any Trainer worth their Rare Candy will know, every great journey begins with your starter Pokémon. After customizing your avatar and meeting Professor Willow, he'll tell you there are three Pokémon in your immediate area. These are your three default starter options: Charmander, Squirtle and Bulbasaur.

There are eighteen different types of Pokémon overall, including 'Dark' type (although not included in the official release) but you get to make your choice from the three cornerstone elements of the game: Fire, Water and Grass.

CHARMANDER: FIRE
Strong against: Bug, Ice, Grass, and Steel
Weak against: Rock, Ground and Water

SQUIRTLE: WATER
Strong against: fire, rock, and ground
Weak against: grass, electric

BULBASAUR: GRASS
Strong against: water, rock, and ground
Weak against: fire, ice, poison, flying and bug

Making your decision is as easy as tapping whichever one you want to start off your team. Doing so will open up the Camera AR mode, so make sure you allow the app access to your camera so you can catch your very first Pokémon!

THE BASICS OF CATCHING POKÉMON:

1 To catch a Pokémon, you have to toss a Pokéball at it; it's as easy as tapping the Pokéball at the bottom of your screen and flicking it towards the Pokémon.

2 Every Pokémon has a coloured circle. Green circles are easy to catch, yellow are medium and red are a little harder. Later in the game, you might have to use some more heavy-duty balls to catch yellow and red circled Pokémon, but since all your starter options are green, a regular Pokéball will get the job done.

FIRST POKÉMON

3

When you tap the Pokéball, the coloured circle will start shrinking. The smaller the circle, the less likely the Pokémon will break free from the ball, so wait until it shrinks down to avoid wasting Pokéballs!

GOTCHA!

Congratulations, you just nabbed yourself the first of what is sure to be many in your journey. You'll be rewarded with some experience points, Stardust and some Candies for your efforts and the praise of Professor Willow, who prompts you to pick a nickname for your avatar. This will be the name you go by for the rest of the game, so choose wisely!

Now that our first buddy is registered in our shiny new Pokédex, it's time to venture out into the big wide world to find it some company. The journey continues...

My Pokédex Notes

TRAINER HACK:

Have you always seen yourself marching through town and taking names with a **Pikachu** by your side? Look no further; it's possible to snag the adorable mascot as your starter Pokémon, too. All you have to do is walk away from all three starter Pokémon (about four or five times should do the trick) for Pikachu to finally pop up.

POKÉSTOPS

Pokéstops are hotspots in your community– buildings, monuments, even art pieces like sculptures and statues - that serve as your port of call when you're roaming the land in your hunt for Pokémon. They provide you with a bunch of useful items essential to your journey, and a little bonus XP for your troubles, too.

Pokéstops are noted on your map with a blue marker. If you're too far away, it will appear as a blue cube. As soon as you get close enough, it will turn into a blue Pokéball. They're pretty impossible to miss on your map.

Once you're close enough, tap on the marker to see a photo of the real-world location. If you swipe on the photo a bunch of items - ranging from Pokéballs, Potions, and even Eggs - will pop up on the screen in little bubbles. Pop the bubbles to claim the lot!

Pokéstop Items

- Pokéballs
- Potions
- Razz Berry
- Revive
- Egg
- Lucky Egg
- Incense
- Great Balls
- Ultra Balls
- Incubators

The higher your level, the more diverse the goodies become.

If you pass level 5 and can start taking on Gyms, you will find the likes of Potions and Revives available to heal your Pokémon. The same rule applies to backpack gear: you're more likely to receive Great Balls and Ultra Balls the higher your Trainer level is.

You should always make a point to stop and swipe at Pokéstops if you see them on your journey. Not only can you pick up some free goodies and replenish your own stock without having to spend any PokéCoins, but the 50 XP you get for every stop you swipe is probably the easiest XP you'll ever earn!

Once you've collected your items, the marker will turn purple, which means you can't use the Pokéstop for a while. No worries! Just wait about five minutes or so for it to refresh again if you need to revisit.

That's an...
interesting Point of Interest!

Pokéstops are classed by Niantic as 'Points of Interest' in the community, which works for big cities with well-known landmarks. However, for more rural areas, it looks like they had to get a little creative with their selections! The game has made a post box, a hamburger door handle and a bench outside a bank Pokéstops; it has even called a bike rack a "Crazy Snake Sculpture."

My Pokédex Notes

TRAINER HACK:
You can place Lure Modules at Pokéstops to draw Pokémon to the area and catch them easily. Check out page 42 for more information on using Lures.

WHAT'S IN YOUR BACKPACK?

Your backpack is filled with everything you'll need on your Pokémon journey.

To check out your backpack, all you have to do is hit the Pokéball in the bottom centre of your screen, then tap 'Items' to bring up the menu.

Your backpack can hold up to 350 items, and whilst that sounds like an awful lot, it can fill up really quickly. There's no point in hoarding Pokéballs or Incense; you'll get the most out of the game if you use them often!

Items

Items are your bread and butter in this game. Be sure to regularly stop by Pokéstops in order to increase your stock and score free items every time you visit. Here are all of the items you can find in game, and why they're useful.

Pokéballs, Great Balls and Ultra Balls

These are your staple items; you can't catch a Pokémon without a Pokéball, after all. If you're running low, you can grab more of these at Pokéstops.

Eggs

These baby Pokémon are ready to hatch, if you're ready to put in the footwork, that is. Check out page 18 to learn more about hatching Eggs.

Lucky Eggs

This item will double any XP you receive for a full thirty minutes. If you're lucky, you'll receive one at a Pokéstop, or as a levelling bonus.

Potions, Super Potions, Hyper Potions and Max Potions

These only come into play after you pass level 5 and start taking on Gyms. As you battle, your Pokémon will likely take a hit or two; Potions will replenish their HP so they can keep going.

Lure Modules

Lures can be placed at Pokéstops and will attract wild Pokémon nearby.

Incense

Incense is very similar to Lures, except they are attached to the Trainer, and not a Pokéstop.

Razz Berries

These little berries can be fed to Pokémon in order to make them easier to catch. If you feed one to a wild Pokémon, their effect will last until you successfully capture it or run from the encounter.

Egg Incubator

These are necessary for hatching Eggs.

Camera

Do you remember Pokémon Snap? Your in-game camera allows you to screenshot any point of the game. Just landed a rare Pokémon? Snap! Spotted a Jigglypuff on the kitchen counter whilst your Mum's cooking dinner? Snap!

Revive and Max Revive

If your Pokémon's HP reaches zero in battle, it will faint. You can't give a fainted Pokémon a Potion; you'll need a Revive to get it back on its feet again.

Most items can be bought in the Shop in exchange for PokéCoins if you can't find them out in the field. You can earn PokéCoins by defending Gyms, but you can also buy them as an in-app transaction. Please make sure you get the bill payer's permission before you attempt any PokéCoin purchases!

How to Use Items

Using items couldn't be easier. Open up your item menu and select the item you wish to use. When you do, it will appear in the in-game window. Tap on it again to confirm that you want to use it. If you've selected the wrong item or swiped by mistake, then just hit 'X' to cancel and return the item to your backpack.

How to Delete Items

If you've just got too many things in your backpack and not enough time to use them all, then you can also simply delete items from your stock. All you have to do is hit the little trashcan symbol next to the item, choose the amount you want to discard and tap 'yes' to confirm.

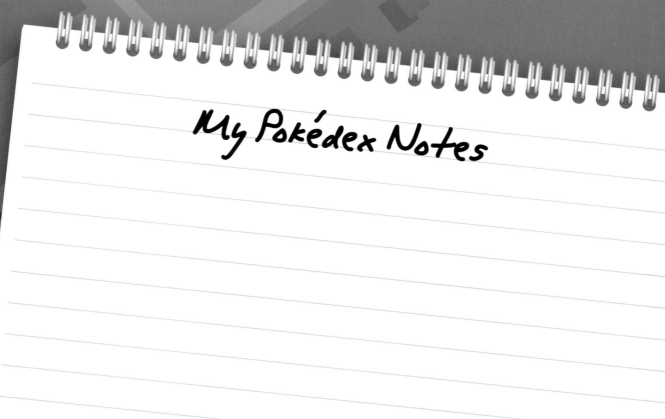

My Pokédex Notes

POWERING UP

Getting stronger has always been a key part of training Pokémon all across the franchise. The traditional way typically involved battling others and gaining experience through victories. If you won enough battles and your Pokémon gained enough experience, they would evolve into a stronger form.

Pokémon Go differs a little in its method. XP earned from playing actually contributes to the Trainer's level, not the Pokémon. In fact, Evolution and Powering Up are two slightly different concepts in this game and neither of them is automatic. Yep, that's right; you have to power up your Pokémon yourself, manually.

Before you start, let's double check you have everything you need:

TRAINER HACK:

Above every Pokémon's picture is a white and grey arc. This is their CP growth potential. When the whole arc is white that means they are maxed out, and cannot be Powered Up any more.

Candy

In order to level up a Pokémon, you will need species-specific Candy. For example, you will need Charmander Candy to feed your Charmander. You can also feed Charmander Candy to another Pokémon in the same evolutionary chain, like Charmeleon or Charizard. You can't give Charmander Candy to, say, Squirtle.

How to get Candy

- Every time you catch a Pokémon, you are rewarded with three Candies for that species.
- You are also rewarded with Candy when you hatch an Egg.
- You can also receive one Candy for every Pokémon you send back to Professor Willow using 'Transfer'. You can find the option at the bottom of your Pokémon's stats page.

Stardust

Stardust is your second essential in Powering up your Pokémon. Unlike Candy, it is not species-specific, so you can use it on any Pokémon you want.

How to get Stardust

- Each time you catch a Pokémon, you will get 100 Stardusts.
- Every time you hatch an Egg, you are also rewarded with some Stardust.
- If you successfully defend your Gym for 21 hours, you will be given a Defender Bonus. This includes PokéCoins and 500 Stardusts.

AND EVOLVING YOUR POKÉMON

You need both Candy and Stardust to successfully Evolve your Pokémon, so make sure you have both before you start to avoid wasting any resources!

Powering Up

In order to Power Up your Pokémon, you need to increase its Combat Power (CP). You will need a certain amount of Stardust and at least one Candy. As expected, the stronger the Pokémon, the more Stardust and Candy you'll need.

Choose the Pokémon, open up their stats page, and then tap Power Up to confirm.

If you have the necessary Items, then it's as easy as that. Keep in mind that a Pokémon's CP actually caps depending on your Trainer level. If you get stronger, so does you Pokémon's capacity for growth.

Evolving

Evolving is similar to Powering Up, except it doesn't require any Stardust. All you need is Candy, but you'll need a lot more of it than just one or two. Most Pokémon need anywhere between 12 and 100 Candies to evolve; if you're trying your luck training a Magikarp, you'll need a whopping 400 Candies before you get your hands on that Gyarados.

TRAINER HACK:

Eeveelution! If you have an Eevee, you can choose the form it will evolve into by changing its name. Choose the Eevee evolution form you want in advance and rename your Eevee "Sparky" for Jolteon, "Pyro" for Flareon, or "Rainer" for Vaporeon. These are the names of the Eevee triplets from the original anime series.

If you have enough Candies for the Evolution, tap "Evolve" and watch the animation. Evolving a Pokémon gives you a sweet 500 XP, and if it's a new Pokémon you haven't caught before, then add an extra 500 XP bonus onto that, too. Congratulations!

EGGS AND INCUBATORS

Eggs

Catching Pokémon in the wild isn't the only way to obtain new entries for your Pokédex. You can also hatch your very own Pokémon by obtaining an Egg. This is a great way to get your hands on some of the Pokémon that are harder to find in your area.

Eggs can be obtained by hitting up your local Pokéstop. Items that are given at Pokéstops are completely random, so you may have to try a few times before you're gifted an Egg. You can keep up to nine Eggs at any one time. There are three different types of Egg: 2 km Eggs, 5 km Eggs and 10 km Eggs.

In order to hatch Eggs, you have to rack up the miles (or kilometres, in this case). There is an in-game tracker that keeps an eye on how much distance you cover whilst playing Pokémon Go. The type of Egg corresponds to the distance in kilometres you will have to walk to hatch it. To hatch a 2 km Egg, you'll need to walk 2 km, for a 5 km Egg, you'll have to log 5 km, and for a 10km Egg? Well, you better be wearing some comfortable shoes!

Incubators

But an Egg and some trainers aren't all that you need. In order for the Egg to actually hatch, you need to put it in an Incubator. If you don't put it in one, none of the distance you walk will count towards hatching.

You start the game with one Incubator - courtesy of Professor Willow's starter pack - but you can also purchase more with PokéCoins, or pick them up at the Pokéstop. There's also a chance you'll receive one as a reward for levelling up. Each Incubator can only hold one Egg at a time.

To use an Incubator, all you have to do is open the Pokémon menu, swipe over to Eggs, and then select the Egg you want to hatch. Tap 'Start Incubation' and you're ready to go.

Note: Professor Willow's Incubator (the orange Incubator; the others are blue) has an infinite amount of uses. Any other Incubator (from the shop or a PokéStop) will break after three uses. It's best then to incubate 2 km Eggs and 5 km Eggs in the Professor Willow's Incubator, and save your other Incubators for 10 km Eggs.

With your Egg in an Incubator, you're ready to go! All you have to do is walk the designated distance and the Egg will hatch. Note the word 'walk'; the game's GPS can detect when you're moving at faster than walking pace, so any distance covered in buses, cars or trains won't count. Make sure you log all your distance on foot if you want to hatch that Pokémon!

Hatching Eggs

You can track your incubation progress at any point by bringing the Eggs menu back up. The Egg will appear in an Incubator and have a little progress bar beneath it, along with the distance required and the distance you've walked so far.

When the Egg hatches, you'll get 200 XP (from a 2km Egg), 500 XP (from a 5km) or a whopping 1000 XP (from a 10km Egg). On top of that, you could also net yourself a 500 XP bonus if the Pokémon is new to your collection. You also get gifted some Pokémon-specific Candies and Stardust.

What's Hiding in There?

It's impossible to choose the Pokémon you're going to get from the Egg, but it is possible to make a safe guess as to what might pop out depending on the Egg type.

Rarer Pokémon become available in 5km Eggs and 10 km Eggs. However, all the other Pokémon available in 2 km Eggs are still in play, so whilst the possibility of a rare Pokémon hatching increases with a longer distance Egg, the chance of it doing so also decreases. You can walk 10km and either hatch a Dratini... or a Weedle. Check out the table to see what kind of Pokémon you can expect from each Egg type.

2 km Egg Pokémon:	5 km Egg Pokémon: (All 2km Pokémon, and...)	10 km Egg Pokémon: (All 2km and 5km Pokémon, and...)
Bulbasaur	Ekans	Onix
Charmander	Sandshrew	Hitmonlee
Squirtle	Nidoran ♀	Hitmonchan
Caterpie	Nidoran ♂	Chansey
Weedle	Vulpix	Scyther
Pidgey	Oddish	Jynx
Magikarp	Paras	Electabuzz
Rattata	Venonat	Magmar
Spearow	Diglett	Pinsir
Pikachu	Meowth	Lapras
Clefairy	Psyduck	Eevee
Jigglypuff	Mankey	Omanyte
Zubat	Growlithe	Kabuto
Geodude	Poliwag	Aerodactyl
	Abra	Snorlax
	Machop	Dratini
	Bellsprout	
	Tentacool	
	Gastly	
	Drowzee	
	Krabby	
	Voltorb	
	Exeggcute	
	Cubone	
	Lickitung	
	Koffing	
	Rhyhorn	
	Tangela	
	Kangaskhan	
	Horsea	
	Goldeen	
	Staryu	
	Mr. Mime	
	Tauros	
	Porygon	

TRAINER HACK:

The in-game pedometer only works whilst the app is open!

21

QUIZ TIME...

1 What is the Pokémon type with the most Pokédex entries in Pokémon Go?
- a) Water
- b) Poison
- c) Normal

2 How many Pokémon are there in the first generation?
- a) 149
- b) 150
- c) 151

3 What is the first Pokémon in the Pokédex?
- a) Bulbasaur
- b) Squirtle
- c) Charizard

4 What is a Fairy type Pokémon NOT weak against?
- a) Poison
- b) Fighting
- c) Steel

5 What Flying Pokémon is yet to have made a confirmed appearance in game?
- a) Zapdos
- b) Charizard
- c) Aerodactyl

6 Which continent is Mr. Mime currently exclusive to?
- a) Australasia
- b) America
- c) Europe

7 Which Pokémon would a Charmander be most effective against?
- a) Squirtle
- b) Bulbasaur
- c) Geodude

8 What is the Pokémon type with the most Pokédex entries in Pokémon Go?
- a) Ice
- b) Steel
- c) Dark

9 A Gym Leader has a Venomoth! You choose a...
- a) Flying Type
- b) Psychic Type
- c) Grass Type

10 What colour is a Pokéstop marker once you have used it?
- a) Grey
- b) Blue
- c) Purple

You know they say that knowledge is power, right? It's time to see if you're ready to become a Pokémon Master...

11 How many uses does a blue Egg Incubator have?
a) 3
b) 4
c) 5

12 Who is the Team Valor leader?
a) Spark
b) Candela
c) Blanche

13 What item do you need to evolve Pokémon in Pokémon Go?
a) Incense
b) Evolution Stone
c) Candy

14 What is the name of the Professor who starts you on your journey?
a) Professor Willow
b) Professor Oak
c) Professor Tree

15 Which one of these is the strongest Pokéball?
a) Ultra Ball
b) Great Ball
c) Pokéball

16 What item should you use to heal your Pokémon?
a) Candy
b) Lures
c) Potions

17 What item should you use on a Pokémon that has fainted?
a) Potion
b) Revive
c) Stardust

18 What does CP stand for?
a) Climbing Power
b) Combat Power
c) Clefairy Parade

19 What is the biggest Pokémon in the first generation?
a) Snorlax
b) Omanyte
c) Kabutops

20 What is the currency in Pokémon Go?
a) PokéPoints
b) PokéPounds
c) PokéCoins

See answers on p.62-63

All of the 151 Pokémon out there to get your hands on fall into different categories, or types.

A Pokémon's type primarily affects its strengths and weaknesses in battle. Most importantly for you eager collectors, it also determines where it is likely to be found on the world map.

GROUND

GROUND POKÉMON: Sandshrew (027), Sandslash (028), Nidoqueen (031), Nidoking (034), Diglett (050), Dugtrio (051), Geodude (074), Graveler (075), Golem (076) Onix (095), Cubone (104), Marowak (105), Rhyhorn (111), Rhydon (112)

Ground types are definitely some of the offensively strongest the game has to offer. They're super effective against five different types of Pokémon (a number matched only by the Fighting type).

It's super effective!
Fire, Electric, Poison, Rock, Steel
It's not very effective...
Water, Grass, Ice

WHERE TO FIND THEM: Whilst you would maybe expect Ground types to live largely in muddy places, they have been spawning in a lot of urban areas, like car parks, roads and railway stations. Quite a few have also been spotted in more expected locations like near streams and open land, but also the less expected, like airports.

24

WATER POKÉMON: Squirtle (007), Wartortle (008), Blastoise (009), Psyduck (054), Golduck (055), Poliwag (060), Poliwhirl (061), Poliwrath (062), Tentacool (072), Tentacruel (073), Slowpoke (079), Slowbro (080), Seel (086), Dewgong (087), Shellder (090), Cloyster (091), Krabby (098), Kingler (099), Horsea (116) Seadra (117), Goldeen (118), Seaking (119), Staryu (120), Starmie (121), Magikarp (129), Gyrados (130), Lapras (131), Vaporeon (134), Omanyte (138), Omastar (139), Kabuto (140), Kabutops (141)

Water Pokémon are certainly a mixed bag: you have your infamous splashing flops (I'm looking at you, Magikarp) as well as its undeniable powerhouses (like Magikarp's evolved beast form, Gyrados). Blastoise has the second highest Base Defense stats in game, and other Water dual-types (like Poliwrath and Omastar) are also excellent defenders.

It's super effective! Water, Ground, Rock
It's not very effective... Ice, Poison, Flying, Bug

WHERE TO FIND THEM: I hope you like swimming! No, don't worry; you don't have to dive in to catch any of these Pokémon, but it's easy enough to track them down near any body of water in the area. Water types can be found around rivers, lakes, harbours and canals, and are even known to frequent a park pond or two every now and then.

WATER

here are a massive eighteen different types of Pokémon out there to grab, and ome of them are dual-types, which means the Pokémon has both a primary and a secondary type to keep in mind when facing it. So let's dive in to the ins-and-outs of Pokémon types.

FIRE

Pokédex Entries: 12

FIRE POKÉMON: Charmander (004), Charmeleon (005), Charizard (006), Vulpix (037), Ninetales (038), Growlithe (058), Arcanine (059), Ponyta (077), Rapidash (078), Magmar (126), Flareon (136), Moltres (146)

Fire Pokémon have always been a popular choice since day one thanks to a certain little lizard with its burning tail, and have continued their streak throughout the years with a number of fan favourite Pokémon to its name. Arcanine, Flareon and Magmar are all in the top 10 Pokémon with the highest Base Attack stats, so they're definitely a smart choice to have in your front line when you challenge gyms.

It's super effective! Steel, Bug, Ice, Grass
It's not very effective... Rock, Water, Ground

WHERE TO FIND THEM: Since locating the nearest volcano to your location is out of the question, you have to be a little creative in matching their game world habitats to your real world counterparts. Fire Pokémon generally tend to be in residential areas and cities, and seem to have a higher spawn rate in neighborhoods. They also pop up in dry/warmer places like beaches and parks.

Pokédex Entries: 14

GRASS POKÉMON: Bulbasaur (001), Ivysaur (002), Venusaur (003), Oddish (043), Gloom (044), Vileplume (045), Paras (046), Parasect (047), Bellsprout (069), Weepinbell (070), Victreebell (071), Exeggcute (102), Exeggutor (103), Tangela (114)

Grass type Pokémon may have the some of the most weaknesses in-game, but don't count them out! Many Grass types are dual-type Pokémon, often with Bug (like the Paras evolutionary chain) and Poison (like the Bellsprout evolutionary chain), so they often have a fair few tricks up their sleeves. On top of that, Exeggutor is in the top 10 Pokémon for both the highest CP and Base Attack stats, so they know how to pack a punch, too.

It's super effective! Water, Ground, Rock
It's not very effective... Ice, Poison, Flying, Bug

WHERE TO FIND THEM: Go green! Grass Pokémon are some of the easiest to track down since they spawn pretty much anywhere there is grass or plants, like parks, farmland and woodland. If you live in the city it might be a bit harder to track down a green grassy field, so try your luck in playgrounds and gardens.

GRASS

25

POKÉMON

NORMAL

Pokédex Entries: 22

NORMAL POKÉMON: Pidgey (016), Pidgeotto (017), Pidgeot (018), Rattata (019), Raticate (020), Spearow (021), Fearow (022), Jigglypuff (039), Wigglytuff (040), Meowth (052), Persian (053), Farfetch'd (083), Doduo (084), Dodrio (085), Lickitung (108), Chansey (113), Kangaskhan (115), Tauros (128), Ditto (132), Eevee (133), Porygon (137), Snorlax (143)

Normal type Pokémon are actually the most common in the game. Whilst they might not have the flashy moveset or special abilities of other types, they are always a solid addition to any team. In fact, Normal type heavyweight Snorlax is one of the strongest Pokémon in game.

It's super effective! None
It's not very effective... Fighting

WHERE TO FIND THEM: You will never have to look too far to find a Normal type Pokémon; chances are there will be around five Rattatas lurking outside your front door right now. Unlike other types, they don't have a particular affinity to any area, and you will likely find some variety of them wherever you go.

ELECTRIC

Pokédex Entries: 09

ELECTRIC POKÉMON: Pikachu (025), Raichu (026), Magnemite (081), Magneton (082), Voltorb (100), Electrode (101), Electabuz (125), Jolteon (135), Zapdos (145)

There aren't all that many electric types in the first generation, but everyone knows Pokémon's number one adorable yellow mascot: Pikachu. Electric types have their signature Thunderbolt attack to handle most battles, but avoid using them to fight against Ground types.

It's super effective! Flying
It's not very effective... Ground

WHERE TO FIND THEM: Electric type Pokémon can be found hanging around industrial areas in the city, like school campuses and industrial parks. Think concrete over greenery.

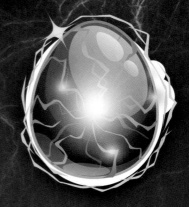

FAIRY

FAIRY POKÉMON: Clefairy (035), Clefable (036), Jigglypuff (039), Wigglytuff (040), Mr. Mime (122)

Fairy Pokémon bring a cheer, an enchantment or two and an unmissable hue of pink into our team. There are actually only two pure Fairy type Pokémon in game: Clefairy and Clefable. The other three entries are dual-types with Fairy as their secondary.

It's super effective! Fighting, Dragon, Dark
It's not very effective... Steel, Poison

WHERE TO FIND THEM: Since Fairy types are a little bit special, they only spawn near local landmarks. In the original Poké region of Kanto, Clefairy could be found on Mt. Moon; in the real world, Clefairy spawn more often in the evening.

POSION POKÉMON: Bulbasaur (001), Ivysaur (002), Venusaur (003), Weedle (013), Kakuna (014), Beedrill (015), Ekans (023), Arbok (024), Nidoran (029), Nidorina (030), Nidoqueen (031), Nidoran ♂ (032), Nidorino ♀ (033), Nidoking (034), Zubat (041), Golbat (042), Oddish (043), Gloom (044), Vileplume (045), Venonat (048), Venomoth (049), Bellsprout (069), Weepinbell (070), Victreebel (071), Tentacool (072), Tentacruel (073), Grimer (088), Muk (089), Gastly (092), Haunter (093), Gengar (094), Koffing (109), Weezing (110)

Whilst they may not be the most psychically imposing, Poison type Pokémon are the perfect pick for the strategic Trainer to gradually weaken their enemies over the course of the battle. Poison is actually the most common type in game, as many Pokémon (particularly Bug and Grass) have poisonous attacks in their secondary type.

It's super effective! Grass, Fairy
It's not very effective... Ground, Psychic

WHERE TO FIND THEM: Luckily you don't have to explore anywhere too toxic to find these creatures. Just look out for wetland areas, like ponds, lakes and marshes, and you'll likely come across a poisonous type or two. They've also been spotted in the odd industrial area too.

POISON

POKÉMON

PSYCHIC

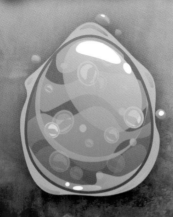

Pokédex Entries: 14

PSYCHIC POKÉMON: Abra (063), Kadabra (064), Alakazam (065), Slowpoke (079), Slowbro (080), Drowzee (096), Hypno (097), Exeggcute (102), Exeggutor (103), Starmie (121), Mr. Mime (122), Jynx (124), Mewtwo (150), Mew (151)

Psychic is one of the rarer types of Pokémon in Pokémon Go. Of the fourteen Pokémon that fall under this category, only half are actually purely psychic type.

Of course, the strongest (and arguably most iconic) of the first generation Pokémon are both psychic; however, Mewtwo and Mew have yet to be found in game.

It's super effective! Fighting, Poison
It's not very effective... Bug, Dark, Ghost

WHERE TO FIND THEM: Finding psychic Pokémon is more of a wildcard than tracking other types. There seems to be a higher chance of coming across them in residential areas at night time. Oddly enough, they've also been spotted around hospitals.

BUG

Pokédex Entries: 12

BUG POKÉMON: Caterpie (010), Metapod (011), Butterfree (012), Weedle (013), Kakuna (014), Beedrill (015), Paras (046) Parasect (047), Venonat (048), Venomoth (049), Scyther (123), Pinsir (127)

Whilst bug types aren't the strongest Pokémon they are some of the cutest critters available to bring into your party. Bug Pokémon tend to shine the most when they are dual type; crossed with flying or poison, they get a whole new buffer to up their battle game.

It's super effective! Grass, Psychic, Dark
It's not very effective... Fire, Rock, Flying

WHERE TO FIND THEM: Bug type Pokémon are super similar to their Grass type pals. Just seek out some greenery and you'll likely stumble across a Caterpie or two. Parks, nature reserves and farmland are all excellent spots for Bug types to spawn.

TYPES

Pokédex Entries: 11

ROCK POKÉMON: Geodude (074), Graveler (075), Golem (076), Onix (095), Rhyhorn (111), Rhydon (112), Omanyte (138), Omastar (139), Kabuto (140), Kabutops (141), Aerodactyl (142)

Of all the eleven Rock types available in the first generation, every single one is a dual-type Pokémon. The most common mixes are with Ground and Water, though the rarest of rock Pokémon - Aerodactyl - is an interesting mix of Rock and Flying.

It's super effective! Fire, Ice, Flying, Bug
It's not very effective... Water, Grass, Fighting, Ground, Steel

WHERE TO FIND THEM: Rock type Pokémon generally spawn near rocks (go figure). Places like hiking trails and quarries are quite popular, but they have been known to appear in more urban areas like car parks and train stations, too.

Pokédex Entries: 08

FIGHTING POKÉMON: Mankey (056), Primeape (057), Poliwrath (062), Machop (066), Machoke (067), Machamp (068), Hitmonlee (106), Hitmonchan (107)

Fighting Pokémon are powerhouses. They're a great addition to any team, especially if you're defending a Gym; Hitmonchan and Poliwrath are two of the best defenders in the game. Only one of the eight fighting Pokémon are dual types, with Poliwrath also bringing some water-based moves to its arsenal.

It's super effective!
Normal, Ice, Rock, Dark, Steel
It's not very effective... Flying, Psychic, Fairy

WHERE TO FIND THEM: In order to recruit some fighters, you're going to have to witness the fitness and get yourself out to your local sports centre or Gym. It makes sense that these physical powerhouses would spawn in sporty places, so also keep an eye out around stadiums.

29

FLYING

FLYING POKÉMON: Charizard (006), Butterfree (012), Pidgey (016), Pidgeotto (017), Pidgeot (018), Spearow (021), Fearow (022), Zubat (041), Golbat (042), Farfetch'd (083), Doduo (084), Dodrio (085), Scyther (123), Gyarados (130), Aerodactyl (142), Articuno (144), Zapdos (145), Moltres (146), Dragonite (149)

Flying type Pokémon are a real mixed bag. All nineteen are dual types, with Fire, Bug, Normal, Poison, Electric, Dragon, Rock and Ice being thrown into the mix. Whichever you choose, know that flying Pokémon have a major advantage against any Ground-type offensive moves.

It's super effective! Grass, Fighting, Bug
It's not very effective… Electric, Ice, Rock

WHERE TO FIND THEM: As we said before, all of the Flying type Pokémon are dual types, so you will find them wherever their second type likes to hang out (i.e. look for Gyarados near water, and Butterfree near grass). They can also generally be found in parks and other grassy areas.

GHOST POKÉMON: Gastly (092), Haunter (093), Gengar (094)

Despite being one of the smallest categories, the Gastly evolutionary chain that makes up the first generation Ghost type Pokémon is certainly one of the most popular. These purple ghouls are more pranksters than horror but they're a great addition to your team nonetheless.

It's super effective! Psychic, Ghost
It's not very effective… Ghost, Dark

WHERE TO FIND THEM: Okay, first things first: despite rumours, you're not more likely to find Ghost types in cemeteries, alright? In fac they lurk around the most regular of corners and can be found in most residential areas, just after the twilight, to add a little spooky edge to your hunt.

GHOST

TYPES

Pokédex Entries: 03

DRAGON POKÉMON: Dratini (147), Dragonair (148), Dragonite (149)

Dragon is another type represented by a single evolutionary chain - shout out to Dratini for flying the flag - but it should certainly be one of the most covetable. Dragonite (Dratini's final form) is currently the strongest Pokémon in the game (it has the highest CP), since legendaries Mewtwo and Mew aren't yet available.

It's super effective! Dragon
It's not very effective... Ice, Dragon, Fairy

WHERE TO FIND THEM: Like Fairy type Pokémon, Dragon types are a little rarer to find, so you will have to go to local landmarks or famous locations if you want to try to find one. Anywhere landmark significant enough to be marked on a map is your best bet.

Pokédex Entries: 02

STEEL POKÉMON: Magnemite (081), Magneton (082)

At the moment, there are only two Steel type Pokémon in game, and Steel is only their secondary type. There are a ton of other Steel type Pokémon in future generations, so it's likely this type will grow in strength as Niantic releases updates and expands the in-game universe over time.

It's super effective! Fairy, Ice, Rock
It's not very effective... Fighting, Fire, Ground

WHERE TO FIND THEM: Since Steel is only a secondary type, you can find Magnemite and Magneton in areas you'd find Electric Pokémon. Check out industrial areas in the city, like schools and industrial parks.

STEEL

31

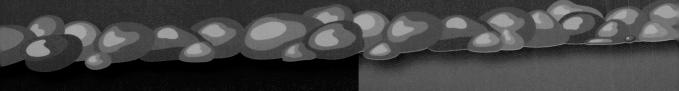

ICE

Pokédex Entries: 05

ICE POKÉMON: Dewgong (087), Cloyster (091), Jynx (124), Lapras (131), Articuno (144)

Ice type Pokémon are all dual type, bringing Water, Psychic and even Flying into play. They're well known in the animé - with Jynx, Lapras and Articuno being some of the most recognisable Pokémon - but a little rarer in game. Unfortunately Lapras isn't able to swim you across any oceans to find any region-exclusives. Not yet, anyway.

It's super effective!
Dragon, Flying, Grass, Ground
It's not very effective…
Fighting, Fire, Steel, Rock

WHERE TO FIND THEM: Thankfully you won't need to crack out your thermals to go hunting for a Dewgong. You should be able to track down Ice types near bodies of water and sometimes even in grassy areas. If you're lucky enough to be near some snow or ice, then you'll be able to find some there, too.

Pokédex Entries: 00

DARK POKÉMON: Gastly (092), Haunter (093), Gengar (094)

There are currently no Dark type Pokémon available, since the game launched with Pokémon's first generation of creatures. However, some code has been found suggesting it is present in game, and there are plenty of Dark type Pokémon in later generations. Perhaps they're coming in a future update?

At the present time, however, we still have some Dark type moves that Pokémon of other types are able to perform.

Dark Pulse
Bite
Feint Attack
Sucker Punch
Night Slash

It's super effective! Ghost, Psychic
It's not very effective: Fire, Flying, Rock

DARK

POKÉMON TYPES

	NOT VERY EFFECTIVE	SUPER EFFECTIVE
NORMAL	Fighting	
FIRE	Rock, Ground	Grass, Ice, Bug, Steel
WATER	Electric, Grass	Fire, Ground, Rock
GRASS	Ice, Bug, Flying, Poison, Fire	Water, Ground, Rock
ELECTRIC	Ground	Flying, Water
ICE	Steel, Rock, Fighting, Fire	Grass, Ground, Flying, Dragon
FIGHTING	Flying, Psychic, Fairy	Normal, Ice, Rock, Dark, Steel
POISON	Ground, Psychic	Grass, Fairy
GROUND	Water, Ice, Grass	Fire, Electric, Poison, Rock, Steel
FAIRY	Poison, Steel	Fighting, Dragon, Dark
FLYING	Electric, Ice, Rock	Grass, Fighting, Bug
PSYCHIC	Bug, Ghost, Dark	Fighting, Poison
BUG	Fire, Flying, Rock	Grass, Psychic, Dark
ROCK	Water, Grass, Fighting, Ground, Steel	Fire, Ice, Flying, Bug
GHOST	Ghost, Dark	Psychic, Ghost
DRAGON	Ice, Dragon, Fairy	Dragon
DARK	Fighting, Bug, Fairy	Psychic, Ghost
STEEL	Fire, Fighting, Ground	Ice, Rock, Fairy

HIDE AND SEEK

In your quest to expand your Pokédex, you will undoubtedly notice that it is harder to come across certain Pokémon than others. There will always be a Rattata around every corner and a Pidgey hovering over your head every ten seconds or so but some of the strongest Pokémon are the most elusive. So, where can you get your hands on some of the game's rarest catches?

Evolution

There are some Pokémon that are certainly harder to find, but by no means impossible. Pokémon like Charizard, Blastoise and Venusaur very rarely appear in the wild, and have to be obtained via Evolution. Check out our guide to Evolving your Pokémon on page 17 for more info.

Regional Rarities

In the original animé, Ash and his friends spend the vast majority of their journey travelling from town to town, city to city and even region to region in their hunt. So it makes sense that Niantic chose to incorporate a little of that into their real world augmented reality. There are four Pokémon - Kangaskhan, Tauros, Farfetch'd and Mr. Mime - that are region exclusives, and can only be found in certain parts of the world.

However, these Pokémon are only region exclusive for wild encounters. There's a slim chance - an extremely slim chance, but a chance nonetheless - that you can still obtain one of these from hatching a 10 km Egg. Of course, you could incubate a thousand 10 km Eggs and end up with a thousand Magikarps (sorry in advance), but hey, Tauros popping out is still a possibility. For more details on eggs and incubators, check out page 18.

My Pokédex Notes

TRACKING DOWN THE GAME'S RAREST CATCHES

KANGASKHAN:
What real-world animal does Kangaskhan look like? And where can you find kangaroos? That's right: Australia! Well, Kangaskhan can be found in Australasia to be exact. It'll be hopping all over the outback, so keep an eye out.

TAUROS:
It makes sense that this Pokémon only hangs out in the country that graced us all with mechanical bulls, right? Okay, it's a stretch, but Tauros is only available in North America. It's a fairly common find on American soil.

FARFETCH'D:
This Normal-Flying dual-type bird can only be found in Asia, with a ton of sightings in Japan and South Korea to confirm. Why Asia? It's all in the name. Farfetch'd is believed to come from a Japanese saying that translates to 'a duck comes bearing green onions.'

MR. MIME:
This marmite Pokémon (you either love him or you hate him, let's be honest) is a European exclusive, and has even been spotted in the middle of London. Why he pops up in Europe isn't all that obvious compared to the other exclusives… maybe our undying love for the art of mime? Hmm. A mystery for the ages.

Come Out, Come Out, Wherever You Are…
So far, no one has reported any sightings of six Pokémon: the two first gen linchpins, Mew and Mewtwo; the three legendary birds, Moltres, Zapdos and Articuno, and everyone's favourite morphable blob of pink goo, Ditto. Data has been found by digging around the game's nuts and bolts that suggests they will make an appearance at some point down the line. Let's keep our fingers crossed in the meantime.

I DIDN'T EXPECT TO SEE YOU HERE...

Where was the weirdest place you've found a Pokémon? Pokémon appear when you least expect it, and in these cases, it's certainly safe to say no one had banked on having to crack open their backpack and grab the nearest Pokéball.

Iraq:

A US marine snapped his discovery of a Squirtle that popped up unexpectedly on the Mosul front line by Teleskuf.

The White House:

There's a Gym located right at the White House in Washington D.C. Previous Gym leaders included a Pidgeot named MERIC

TRAINER HACK:

Many rare Pokémon appear near local landmarks, but the game's definition of 'point of interest' certainly has some variety to it. Try looking out local landmarks to find some more unexpected Pokémon in unexpected places!

Baseball Games:

There have been numerous accounts of Pokémon making unexpected appearances in the middle of baseball games in the US. Lickitung, Magikarp and Krabby have all been spotted centre field.

CAPTURING POKEMON WHEN YOU LEAST EXPECT IT!

SS Alkimos:
The shipwreck SS Alkimos lies to the coast north of Perth, Australia, and is a designated Pokémon Gym. Can you fit a kayak in your backpack?

Picking Fights at Sega:
Nintendo (the original creators of Pokémon) and Sega have been rival companies for decades, but did you know there's currently a Pokémon Gym stationed in the Sega HQ in Japan?

DRAW YOUR OWN
POKÉMON!

Brand new and exciting Pokémon are being released every generation, from fairy bulldogs and ninja frogs to ghost chandeliers and killer ice cream cones! Create your very own Pokémon below and who knows? Maybe something similar will pop up in the next gen!

GOT CHA!

A wild Pokémon has appeared! Can you find the Pokéball quickly enough to catch it?

GO!

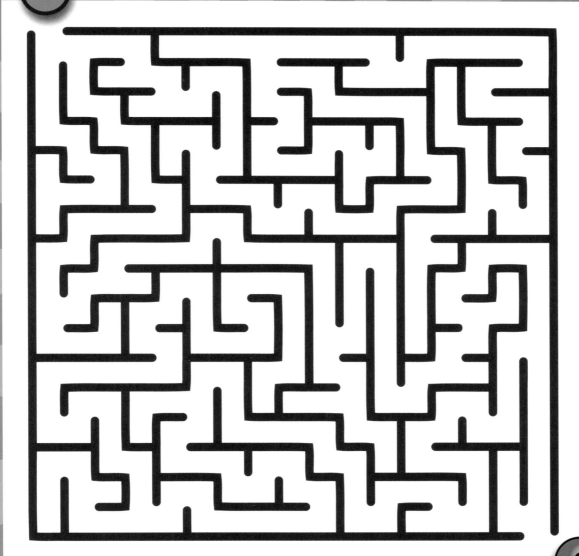

Answers on p.62-63

TIPS AND
FOR IMPROVING

Turn Off AR Mode

When you capture your starter Pokémon, the game asks you to switch on AR mode, which allows you to see the Pokémon in the real world, like by the window, in the park, or on top of an unsuspecting person.

Whilst it will always be novelty to see a Zubat hovering over the park bench, it does make it a little harder to catch them, as you need to move in order to keep the Pokémon in view. This could result in a bunch of wasted Pokéballs being tossed and a lot of frustrated fists being balled up.

If catching Pokémon is proving difficult, switch off AR mode by tapping the button in the top right corner of your screen next time you encounter a wild Pokémon. That will replace the real-world background with a standard greenery image, which fixes the Pokémon centre-screen and makes it easier for you to capture.

Put a Ring On It

Whenever you encounter a wild Pokémon, a coloured ring will start shrinking over the creature. The colours go by the standard traffic light system:

Green: An easy catch, and the Pokémon has relatively low CP.
Yellow: Requires a little more skill, and the Pokémon is maybe a second tier evolution or has higher CP.
Red: A red-ringed Pokémon won't make it an easy task for you, that's for sure. It is either very powerful, or very rare.

TRICKS
YOUR CATCH RATE

These are the three main colours, but you'll also find some Pokémon have rings that are shades in between. For example, a Haunter might pop up with orange circle, meaning it is between Yellow and Red in terms of difficulty. On the other hand, a Yellow-Green circle on a Kakuna means it will be a moderately easy catch.

When the ring is its smallest, toss your ball: the smaller the ring, the bigger the chance of landing the catch!

Throw A Curve Ball

Did you know there is actually more than one way to throw a Pokéball? The Curve Ball technique is hard to master and may only net you a 10 XP bonus, but it has the highest success rate of all the other throws in game. For more information on how to perfect that Curve Ball, check out page 45.

Know Your Pokéballs

Not all Pokémon are created equal. Unfortunately, a regular Pokéball that does a-ok on capturing a Caterpie isn't going to be able to nab a Snorlax with the same effort. Rarer and more powerful Pokémon are best attempted with Great Balls or Ultra Balls to increase the chance of a successful catch.

Lure 'Em In

The simplest way to increase your catch rate is by increasing the number of Pokémon you encounter, right? If you use an item like Incense or a Lure Module, it will attract more Pokémon and give you the chance to take them all on. Check out page 42 on how to use these items correctly.

THERE'S SOMETHING IN THE AIR

Incense and Lure

Both Incense and Lure are designed to attract wild Pokémon. The main difference between the two is that Lures attract Pokémon to a Pokéstop and Incense attracts Pokémon to a Trainer. Everyone can benefit from the draw effect of a Lure, regardless of who set it off. However, Incense is Trainer-specific and can only effect the player. The Pokémon that appear under this effect are generally a little rarer, so it's a great way to get your hands on some of the more elusive creatures in the game. You can tell when either Incense or Lure is in effect by the swirl of pink and purple petals that will appear.

Incense

Professor Willow starts you off with two Incense pots to kick off your journey, and you can find them in your Items Menu. If you need more, you can get them as rewards for Levelling Up, and they are also available to purchase with PokéCoins.

It draws nearby wild Pokémon to you so you don't have to travel so far to find them. Its effect lasts 30 minutes, which continues to count down even when you close the app.

How to use Incense

1. Open your Item Menu by tapping the Pokéball at the bottom of the screen.
2. Find the Incense and tap it.
3. Tap the Incense again when it appears on your main screen.
4. Your 30 minutes start now!

Pokémon that appear whilst you are using Incense are only available to you, so you don't have to worry about chasing them down in a mad rush to beat other trainers nearby.

Incense is way more effective if you keep moving. Staying put with Incense active will still attract Pokémon, but you will attract a lot more by walking around with it on.

Lures

Lures are very similar to Incense, but have a group effect, and can only be used at Pokéstops. They spawn new Pokémon near the Pokéstop's location. Lures can be acquired as rewards for Levelling Up, but you can also buy them in exchange for PokéCoins, too.

How to use Lures

1. Find a Pokéstop and tap on it.
2. Tap the white space under the name.
3. Tap the Lure module, and tap it again.
4. Your 30 minutes start now!

Lures are a good way to make friends with other Trainers in the area. Since your name appears above the Lure you set off, it's an easy way for others to see who made the goodwill gesture to help everyone out.

My Pokédex Notes

TRAINER HACK:

Since you're almost guaranteed to find a constant stream of Pokémon for 30 minutes, using Incense and Lures are super effective ways to gain XP and Level Up quickly. If you also use a Lucky Egg (which doubles your XP gained for 30 minutes), you will be swimming in XP and shooting up the level ranks in no time.

A GUIDE TO POKÉBALLS

Pokéballs are as important to a Trainer as a racket to a tennis player; you can't be a Pokémon Trainer without catching any Pokémon, right? There's nothing more frustrating than wandering the town, stumbling across an elusive Mr. Mime and then looking in your backpack to find you have nothing to capture it with. They're essentials you can't leave home without. Shoes? Check. Phone? Check. Pokéballs? Check. You're good to go.

There are currently three different types of Pokéballs available in game: Pokéballs, Great Balls, and Ultra Balls.

Pokéballs
You will start your journey with a plentiful supply of Pokéballs thanks to Professor Willow, but as you get the hang of perfecting your throws and start capturing different Pokémon left, right and centre, you'll soon find your stock running low. No worries; Pokéballs are easily attainable and can either be found at Pokéstops or purchased with PokéCoins.

Great Balls
Great Balls are the next step up from regular Pokéballs, and have a better chance of capturing the Pokémon on your first throw. However, Great Balls can't be bought like Pokéballs. You can find them at Pokéstops once you hit level 10, or receive them as a levelling bonus.

Ultra Balls
Like Great Balls, Ultra Balls are not available for purchase. Instead, you can find them at Pokéstops (from level 20), or as a reward for Levelling Up. Keep them to toss at some of those red-ringed Pokémon to snare some of the rarer Pokémon for your team.

Master Balls
Okay, okay, Master Balls aren't official just yet. However, there are excited whispers about this legendary Pokéball being present in the game's coding, and speculation that it will become available when Trainers' levels start reaching dizzying heights. Why the hype for some hidden code, you ask? The Master Ball is by far the strongest Pokéball across all of the Pokémon universe (the hint is in the name, right?), with a 100% guaranteed catch rate, even on legendary Pokémon. Time will tell whether this ace will make its appearance or not.

PERFECTING YOUR THROW

Exercise your throwing arm and get acquainted with these catch bonuses.

Nice! Throw your Pokéball inside the coloured ring whilst it's still fairly large. You'll get a 10 XP bonus if you make the catch.

Great! Throw your Pokéball when the coloured ring is about half the size of the white circle. If you're successful, you'll get a 50 XP bonus.

Excellent! Throw your Pokéball when the coloured ring is just about at its smallest. This is by far the hardest toss, and if you pull it off, you'll be rewarded with a 100 XP bonus.

The Elusive Curve Ball

The Curve Ball may only grant you a measly 10 XP bonus, but it does have a way higher success rate of actually landing the catch. If you're sick of wasting Pokéballs with flop throws or you really, really, really want that Ekans, then why not give it a go?

1. Place your finger on the Pokéball and start spinning it. Pay attention to the direction you're spinning: clockwise or anti-clockwise.

2. The ball will start to vibrate and sparkle, that is time to stop spinning and get to tossing. If you spun the ball clockwise, flick the your finger up the left of the screen. If you spun the ball anti-clockwise, then flick it up the right.

It takes some time to master, so don't stress if you don't get it on the first try. With a little practice, soon you'll be throwing curve balls and catching Clefables like a pro.

CAN YOU SOLVE ALL CLUES ON THE CROSSWORD PUZZLE?

ACROSS

1 The yellow electric mouse mascot of Pokémon. (7)

5 The Leader of Team Mystic. (7)

7 A Pokémon type that is weak against Water. (4)

8 The place where all of your items are kept. (8)

10 The item used to evolve a Pokémon. (5)

DOWN

2 Spark is the Leader of this Team. (8)

3 Something you need in order to hatch Eggs. (9)

4 The colour of Team Valor. (3)

6 An item that gives you double XP. (5,3)

9 Something you give yoru Pokémon to replenish its HP. (6)

Answers on p.62-63

```
T A N O N E V L G R K O L
K W R E M W Q M I R D D L
N T U A X Z E S N D R R E
H T A L K E N E I N W E B
H T S E L I G S D E Z H E
T K A G P W H G I L R T E
T A B N S R T P C T E Y R
E K L A K A R J Q U V C T
L U U T D E R N L Y T S C
G N B K T T L A L M P E I
I A B A H G N N P Y V M V
D Y C B U T T E R F R E E
X P Z T U O R P S L L E B
```

FIND THE CHARACTERS BELOW IN THE WORD SEARCH!

Bellsprout

Bulbasaur

Butterfree

Caterpie

Diglett

Exeggcute

Kakuna

Oddish

Paras

Pinsir

Scyther

Tangela

Venonat

Victreebell

Weedle

Answers on p.62-63

HOW TO LEVEL UP

The main difference between Pokémon Go and other entries in the series is that all experience (XP) gained from battles and completing other tasks does not go to your Pokémon, but to the Trainer instead.

Whilst you might think making sure your Pokémon are super-buff and ready to fight is the most important thing, making sure your Trainer level is just as high is way more integral than you'd expect. Your Pokémon's strength and abilities are directly tied to your Trainer's level. They can only increase their CP if you're at a high enough level. Quite simply: if you don't grow, they don't grow.

So what are the best methods for gaining XP? Here are five tips to rake in the XP faster than you can recite all 151 first generation Pokémon from memory (okay... considerably faster).

Tip: The Lucky Egg! If you're looking to really pump up your XP, why not try a Lucky Egg? They double any XP you earn over a period of 30 minutes. You can find these gems randomly at Pokéstops, or purchase them with PokéCoins in the shop.

1. Capture Pokémon
This one's obviously a given, but you've got to try and catch them all if you want to Level Up! There are a bunch of XP bonuses hidden in almost every aspect of catching a Pokémon.

- Nice Throw! Depending on how you throw your Pokéball, you can get anywhere from 10 XP to 100 XP as a bonus. Check out page 45 for more about different Pokéball throws.
- Nice Catch! Every time you successfully catch a Pokémon, you'll get a 100 XP bonus.
- New Pokémon! If the Pokémon you just snagged is a new entry to your Pokédex, you'll also land a 500 XP bonus on top of everything else.

2. Hatch Eggs
Hatching Eggs you find along your journey isn't just a good way to add to your team, but also a good way to buff up your Trainer level.
- Depending on the type of Egg, you will get 200 XP, 500 XP or 1000 XP when it hatches.
- If it's a new Pokémon that hatches, you'll get another 500 XP bonus.

3. Evolve Pokémon
Whilst evolution is strictly for Pokémon (unfortunately there is very little chance of a real-life Magikarp to Gyarados-style transformation), your Trainer can also benefit from the process by gaining some XP.
- When you Evolve any Pokémon from any tier, you will net a 500 XP bonus.
- And yep, you guessed it: if it evolves into a Pokémon you haven't caught before, then add an extra 500 XP bonus.

YOUR TRAINER

4. Hit the Gym

Gyms are a whole other ball game in Pokémon Go compared to other Pokémon games, but they're still key to gaining experience and Levelling Up.

- Training at a friendly Gym will gain you XP for every Pokémon you defeat.
- If you successfully challenge another team's Gym and come out on top, you'll also earn XP for your victory.

5. Visit Pokéstops

This is probably the easiest way to get some XP and fast. Any time you swipe a Pokéstop, you'll get 50 XP for your troubles.

Pokéstops are also excellent for XP farming from capturing Pokémon, as you can benefit from Lure Modules set at them. For more details about Lure Modules, check out page 42 in this guide.

CHOOSING YOUR POKÉMON TEAM

So far, every time you've walked into a Gym, you've been knocked back. But as soon as you hit level five? That is a game changer. At level five, the real competition begins. So you want to emulate Ash Ketchum and be the very best Pokémon Trainer? So does everyone else, and you're going to have to fight them for it.

The first choice you have to make in your journey to the top is deciding what team you want to join. You will represent your team in all of your Gym battles from here on out. Professor Willow will introduce you to his colleagues, each representing one of the teams.

There are three teams (with colours modelled on the three original Pokémon games, and the three first generation legendary birds) to choose from: Mystic, Valor and Instinct.

Mystic

Mascot: Articuno
Leader: Blanche

Team Mystic values the wisdom of Pokémon above all else. The leader, Blanche, researches the secrets behind Pokémon evolution. Their motto is that with calm analysis of battles and situations, they can't lose.

Valor

Mascot: Moltres
Leader: Candela

Team Valor is a fiery team that champions strength. Their leader, Candela, researches ways to enhance Pokémon's natural power. They believe that training and battling are key to becoming the best Pokémon Trainer.

Instinct

Mascot: Zapdos
Leader: Spark

Team Instinct is led by Spark, and thinks both Pokémon and humans have great intuitions. Spark researches Egg incubation and hatching. For Team Instinct, trusting your gut is the secret to victory.

Unsure which one to pick? Why not try out our quiz to find out what team would suit you best? Whatever your answer, take time to think! You can't change your mind and pick a different team after making your decision. Choose carefully!

I CHOOSE YOU!

What is the best way to win a battle?
A: Analysing data
B: Training and strength
C: Trusting your gut

What do you value most?
A: Wisdom
B: Strength
C: Skills

Who is the coolest legendary bird?
A: Articuno
B: Moltres
C: Zapdos

What is your favorite colour?
A: Blue
B: Red
C: Yellow

What starter Pokémon did you choose?
A: Squirtle
B: Charmander
C: Bulbasaur or Pikachu

What's the best way to learn about your Pokémon?
A: Reading about its statistics
B: Training and learning from battle
C: Understanding its strengths and weaknesses

Team Mystic: Mostly As

Team Valor: Mostly Bs

Team Instinct: Mostly Cs

GYM BATTLE

Gyms are the battle arenas of Pokémon Go. You won't be using your team to take on beasts or Trainers out in the wild, but rather to challenge and train at Gyms, all in the name of your team.

It's not hard to track down a Gym: it's the tallest of all the markers on your map. The marker will be one of four colours:

Red: Team Valor controls this Gym.

Blue: Team Mystic controls this Gym.

Yellow: Team Instinct controls this Gym.

Grey: This Gym is currently unclaimed.

If you spot one on your map, tap it to see the name of the landmark location to track it down. You won't be able to enter and battle if you are not within the immediate vicinity.

If a Gym is controlled by an opposing team, you can challenge the Pokémon inside to a battle. Battling in Pokémon Go is a lot more streamlined than in the other Pokémon titles. You don't have a full array of moves to choose from, but you still need to be smart and try to play to type strengths and weaknesses (check out page 24 for more details). You can take up to six Pokémon with you to take on the Gym.

Before you start, be sure to put your Pokémon in the order you would want to fight with. Swapping out Pokémon does not pause the battle, so your enemy will continue to attack and might get the upper hand!

Tip: All battles are timed, and limited to 100 seconds.

Fast Attack!
Tap your Pokémon for a fast attack. Doing this will charge your Special Attack meter.

Dodge!
You can dodge your opponent's moves by swiping either left or right.

Special Attack!
When your Special Attack meter has been charged up, press and hold your Pokémon to perform their special move for more damage.

Try not to use Special Attacks too often! They may look cool and do a lot of damage, but they also leave your Pokémon vulnerable to counters. Make sure you use it when your Pokémon has the upper hand, or to deliver a devastating final blow.

BASICS

Keep an eye on your Pokémon's HP. If it hits zero, your Pokémon will faint, and if all your Pokémon faint, then the battle is over.

If you win, the Gym's allegiance will change from the previous faction to yours. Now that's team work!

Prestige

Like Pokémon and their Trainers, Gyms have their own levels and rank based on their success in battle. This is measured in what is called Prestige. To boost a Gym's Prestige, you just have to train in it, or leave a Pokémon behind to defend it. In order to take over a Gym, you have to reduce its Prestige to zero, and the only way to do that is to defeat all of the Pokémon inside.

If a Gym receives enough Prestige, it will Level Up. The higher a Gym's Level, the more Pokémon that can be left to defend it, which means the harder it is to take down and take over. Every Level the Gym gains means one more Pokémon can stay behind, e.g. at Level 1, one Pokémon can defend the Gym; at Level 2, two Pokémon can defend the Gym.

Gym Level	Prestige Required
1	0
2	2,000
3	4,000
4	8,000
5	12,000
6	16,000
7	20,000
8	30,000
9	40,000
10	50,000

GYM TRAINING

If a Gym is a friendly Gym, (meaning it is controlled by your team), then you can hit it up at any point to train your Pokémon. Do not worry, there is not a cross-trainer or treadmill even vaguely involved in this process, but your thumb might get a good work out from all the tappings its about to do.

You can only take one Pokémon into a Gym at a time to train, so choose carefully!

Why Train?

Training at a friendly Gym has some great benefits, for both you and your team. Every battle you win whilst training, you gain XP as a Trainer. You also contribute to the Gym's overall Prestige, which will help the Gym level up. Snaps for everyone!

Training is the best way to get used to the combat system, and understand the ins and outs of it first-hand. All battles in Pokémon Go are in real-time (unlike previous Pokémon games, which all favour a more strategic turn-based system) so it's key that you know your way around the system comfortably when it comes to challenging opponent-held Gyms later on. Your ability to tap and swipe at the right time is the difference between winning and losing. It's a risk-free way to practice for those fights without having to crack into your Revive stock. Practice makes perfect!

Who Are You Training With?

Your teammates! Whatever Pokémon have been stationed at the Gym by the Gym Leaders (i.e. other players) aren't just there to defend it from would-be challengers but also to spar with you.

TRAINER HACK:

Be smart when picking your battles. Look at your sparring partners' type and try to choose a Pokémon according to its strengths and weaknesses. Also be sure to take note of your opponent's CP. Pokémon with a higher CP will more than likely come out on top; sometimes luck might hand you a victory or two but generally CP is paramount. Sparring in Gyms is a good indicator to see whether your team is the right level to be successfully taking on other Gym-related challenges in your area.

My Pokédex Notes

henever you see a Gym on the map, you'll see its strongest defender Pokémon above the
arker. When you tap on the Gym, you can swipe on the menu that pops up to see the other
okémon that are defending it, too.

ow Do You Train?

ith your battle basics, of course. You can spar amongst your teammates' Pokémon. The higher
e Gym's level, the more Pokémon can be left behind to spar with. Gyms can range from Level
to Level 10, and Pokémon are ordered from the weakest (the lowest CP) to the strongest (the
ghest CP). See the little boxing glove icon in the bottom right of the screen? Tap it to start
parring.

hen you start battling, you'll just fight all of the Gym's stationed Pokémon in succession until
ther you win, or your team's HP reaches zero.

you're struggling to win any battles, your Pokémon team may need buffing up. Check out our
uide on Powering Up and Evolving your Pokémon on page 16.

you keep training and boosting the Gym's Prestige, it might gain enough to Level Up. If a Gym
evels Up, that means it has one new spot for a resident Pokémon…

TRAINER HACK:

Battling at a friendly Gym
means your Pokémon can
still run out of HP, but they
won't faint. That means
you can just use Potions to
perk them up again; you
can save your Revives for
a rainy day.

BECOMING A

This is it. The moment you have been waiting for. The moment you become a Gym Leader!

There are three ways in which you can become a Gym Leader:

1 **If you luck out,** you might come across an unclaimed Gym. Hey, crazier things have happened. If you're lucky enough to find one, you can claim the Gym with your team colours and set up shop as its first Gym Leader.

2 **You can train at a friendly Gym** and contribute to its Prestige. Once a Gym hits a certain level of Prestige, it can Level Up, which creates one new space for a new Pokémon to step in as its defender.

3 **You can challenge an enemy Gym** and battle the defending team repeatedly so the Gym loses its Prestige. If you successfully deplete the Gym's Prestige to zero, it will become unclaimed, and ready for you to take over.

Which Pokémon Should I Choose?

When a spot opens up at the Gym, you will see a small icon in the bottom left of the screen. It has a little Pokéball and a plus symbol, so tap it to add the Pokémon you want to defend the Gym.

You need to choose very carefully which Pokémon you want to leave behind in your stead. You will not be able to change your mind or swap it out for another choice until the challenging team beats you and kicks you out, so your decision is an important one. You can place your Pokémon in up to 10 different Gyms, but you have to be within the range of a Gym to add a Pokémon to it.

Defending Your Gym

The Pokémon you left behind now acts as your representative at that Gym. Other team members can train and spar with it, and of course, that means opposing teams can also challenge it. If an opposing team member challenges the Gym, you will not have to fight the player. Instead, your Pokémon will be controlled by AI; you will only know the outcome of the match if

My Pokédex Notes

GYM LEADER

you have your Pokémon returned to you with 1HP (that means you lost and got kicked out) or if you are eligible to collect a Defender Bonus from the Shop.

Defender Bonus
Once you've stationed your Pokémon in a Gym, you'll earn a daily bonus defending it. This is called the Defender Bonus, and you can collect it every 21 hours. Bring up the Shop menu (via your Pokéball in the bottom centre of your screen), and you'll notice a little shield icon in the top right corner. Tap it to collect your Bonus.

For every Pokémon that has successfully defended a Gym for 21 hours, you will receive 500 Stardust and 10 PokéCoins. That means you can get up to 5,000 Stardust and 100 PokéCoins for having 10 Pokémon defending Gyms!

Defender Bonuses are the only way to earn PokéCoins in game without requiring an in-app transaction, so it's a good idea to challenge as many Gyms as you can so you can get your Pokémon stationed in and earning their keep!

TRAINER HACK:
Only Pokémon with full HP can be left behind as a defender.

Be sure to leave behind one of your stronger teammates, but not your strongest. You'll still need a Pokémon on your side to challenge and conquer new Gyms that you find, so you don't want to leave behind your ace and then spend hours and hours retraining your team from scratch.

WINNING MEDALS

So you're filling up your Pokédex and racking up the miles, but what's the point of being the very best (that no one ever was) if you don't have the shiny hardware to prove it? Pokémon Go has a number of different Medals you can earn to show off your various in-game achievements.

You'll probably find yourself stumbling upon a few medals just by simply playing your way through the game and catching Pokémon, but if you're actively trying to go for gold, then here is a guide to earning all of the currently available medal achievements in Pokémon Go.

Medal Name	Requirements	Bronze Requirement	Silver Requirement	Gold Requirement
Jogger	Walk a certain distance	10 km	100 km	1,000 km
Kanto	Register Pokédex entries	5	50	100
Collector	Capture Pokémon	30	500	2000
Scientist	Evolve Pokémon	3	20	200
Breeder	Hatch eggs	10	100	1000
Backpacker	Visit Pokéstops	100	1,000	2,000
Battle Girl	Win Gym battles	10	100	1,000
Ace Trainer	Train at your Gym	10	100	1,000
Kindler	Catch Fire Pokémon	10	50	200
Swimmer	Catch Water Pokémon	10	50	200
Gardener	Catch Grass Pokémon	10	50	200
Rocker	Catch Electric Pokémon	10	50	200
Schoolkid	Catch Normal Pokémon	10	50	200
Black Belt	Catch Fighting Pokémon	10	50	200
Punk Girl	Catch Poison Pokémon	10	50	200
Hiker	Catch Rock Pokémon	10	50	200
Bug Catcher	Catch Bug Pokémon	10	50	200
Bird Keeper	Catch Flying Pokémon	10	50	200
Ruin Maniac	Catch Ground Pokémon	10	50	200
Hex Maniac	Catch Ghost Pokémon	10	50	200
Fairy Tale Girl	Catch Fairy Pokémon	10	50	200
Psychic	Catch Psychic Pokémon	10	50	200
Dragon Tamer	Catch Dragon Pokémon	10	50	200
Skier	Catch Ice Pokémon	10	50	200
Depot Agent	Catch Steel Pokémon	10	50	200
Pikachu Fan	Catch Pikachu	3	50	300
Fisherman	Catch large Magikarps	3	50	300
Youngster	Catch small Rattatas	3	50	300

I DIDN'T EXPECT TO SEE YOU HERE...

Where was the weirdest place you've found a Pokémon? It seems Pokémon have enjoyed exploring London just as much as the tourists do!

Buckingham Palace:

Players have found Psychic type Pokémon wandering inside the gates of Buckingham Palace. Both Jynx and Drowzee were spotted trying to make a visit to the Queen.

TRAINER HACK:

If you're playing in London, be sure to check out the area near Central. All of the Pokéstops there are a real Lure Module Hotspot!

Downing Street:

Whilst a BBC reporter was waiting for Theresa May to ma her first appearance as Prime Minister, he spotted a Pika waiting outside Downing Street too. There was also a Drowzee hanging around outside the Chancellor's hous

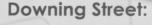

CAPTURING POKÉMON WHEN YOU LEAST EXPECT IT!

MI5

Did you know there is a Gym inside the MI5 building? Are they training up Pokémon along with super spies now, too? Who knows!

Big Ben:

There's also a Gym inside Big Ben! Is Pokémon getting Political? Pikachu for Prime Minister!

London Wall:

The Museum of London tweeted a snapshot of a Krabby hanging out by the historical London Wall.

P.22 QUIZ ANSWERS

1.	B		11.	A
2.	C		12.	B
3.	A		13.	C
4.	B		14.	A
5.	A		15.	A
6.	C		16.	C
7.	B		17.	B
8.	C		18.	B
9.	A		19.	A
10.	C		20.	C

P.39 WILD TRAINER MAZE

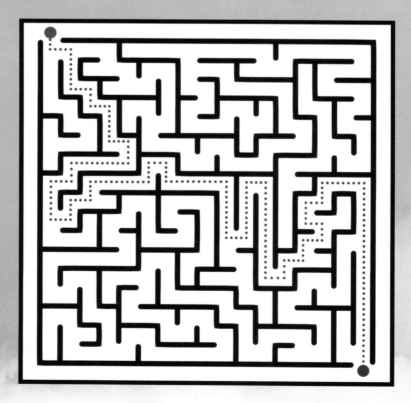